ANCIENT EGYPT

First published in Great Britain in 2003 by
The British Museum Press
A division of the British Museum Company Ltd
46 Bloomsbury Street, London WC1B 3QQ

ISBN 0 7141 3025 7

Everyday Life in Ancient Egypt
was created and produced by McRae Books
Borgo Santa Croce, 8 – Florence (Italy)
e-mail: info@mcraebooks.com

SERIES EDITOR Anne McRae
TEXT Neil Morris
ILLUSTRATIONS Daniela Astone, Manuela Cappon, Luisa Della Porta, Sauro Giampaia, Paola Ravaglia, Andrea Ricciardi di Gaudesi, Studio Stalio (Alessandro Cantucci, Fabiano Fabbrucci, Andrea Morandi)
GRAPHIC DESIGN Marco Nardi
LAYOUT Laura Ottina, Adriano Nardi
EDITING Susan Kelly, Anne McRae
REPRO Litocolor, Florence
PICTURE RESEARCH Susan Kelly

Printed and bound in Belgium

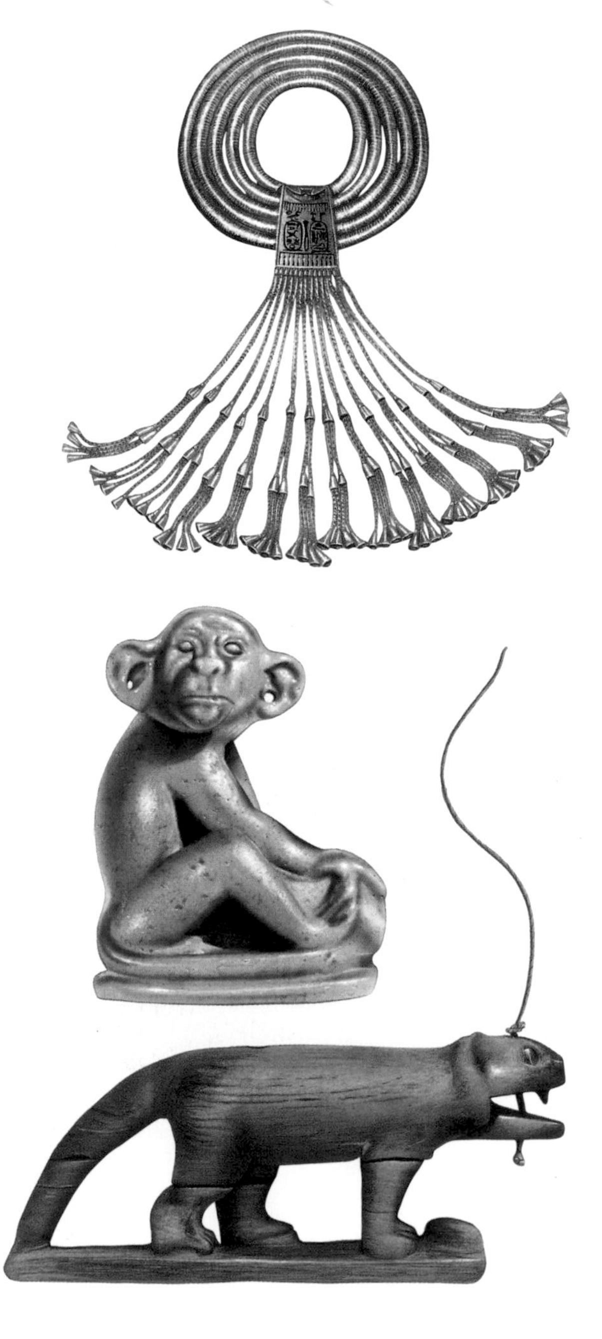

Neil Morris

ANCIENT EGYPT
EVERYDAY LIFE IN

Illustrations by Daniela Astone, Manuela Cappon,
Luisa Della Porta, Sauro Giampaia, Studio Stalio

THE BRITISH MUSEUM PRESS

Table of Contents

Introduction

The land of Egypt was home to one of the greatest civilizations of the ancient world. After the two lands of Upper and Lower Egypt united around 3150 BC, the kingdom flourished along the banks of the Nile River for almost 3,000 years. As small settlements turned into villages, and then grew into thriving towns, the Egyptians constructed grand monuments such as tombs for their kings and temples for their gods. Many of these buildings – along with well-preserved coffins, mummies, wall paintings, and statues – have been uncovered, and they tell us about the lives of the pharaohs and their royal families. The ancient Egyptians' famous constructions are among the wonders of the ancient world. But Egypt's dry climate also helped to preserve many other objects down the centuries, long after they were no longer used. In recent times, archaeologists have learned more about the ancient Egyptians by uncovering and investigating the houses, villages, and everyday objects they left behind. These discoveries have thrown light on the beliefs and lives of ordinary people, including traders, craftspeople, artists, builders, and the many farmers who used the annual Nile flood to produce the crops and food that provided the basis for the civilization of ancient Egypt.

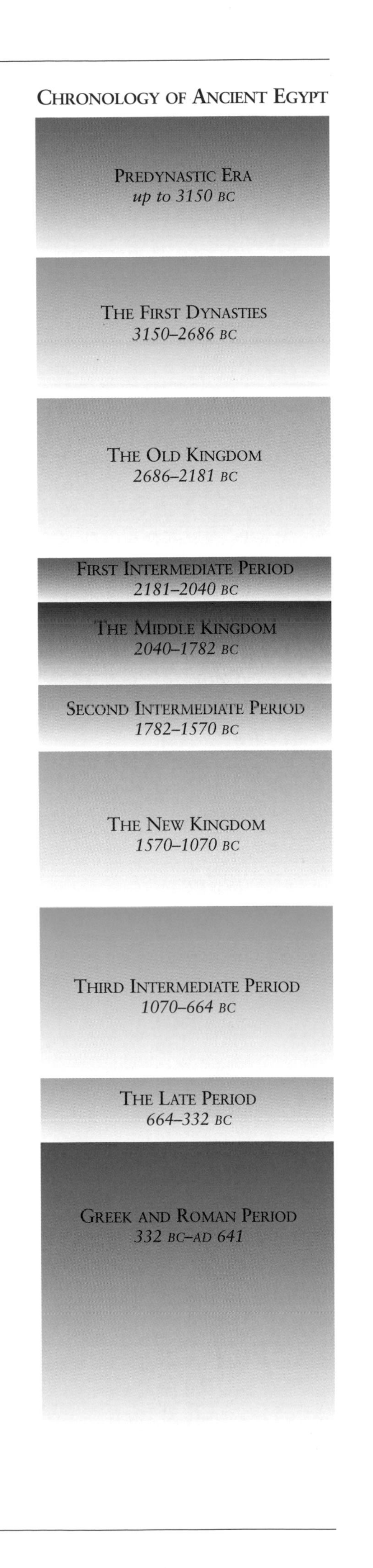

Predynastic Egypt

The period of very early Egyptian history, from about 5500 to 3150 BC, is called 'predynastic' because it came before the dynasties of ruling families reigned over a united Egypt. Even before this time hunter-gatherers had settled in the region, and their tiny farming settlements gradually grew into villages. They eventually formed two kingdoms: Lower Egypt, which covered the lowlands of the Nile Delta, and Upper Egypt, which was a narrow strip of fertile land further up the Nile valley. As their kingdoms flourished, the early Egyptians became skilled craftworkers. We have found some of their art and crafts in graves and tombs, where they were placed to accompany the dead into the next life.

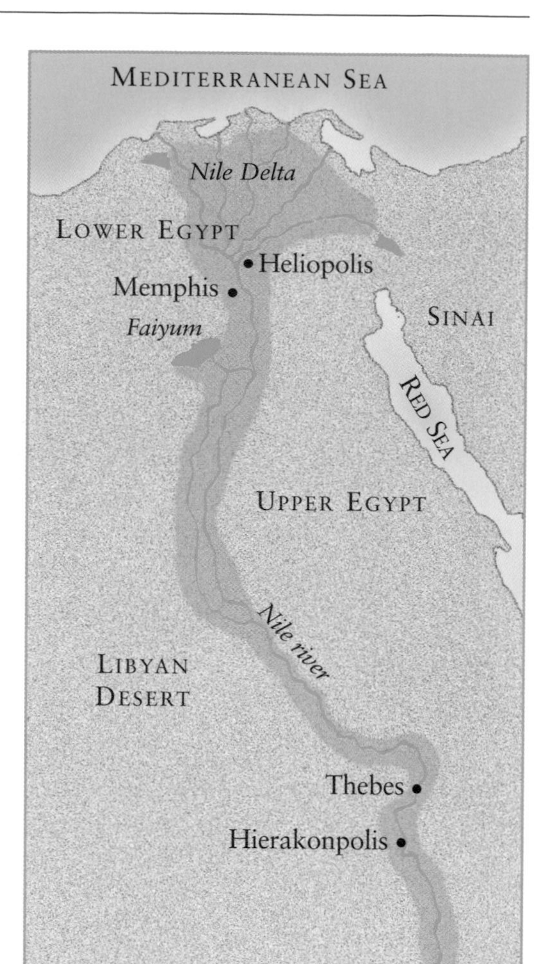

Settling the Nile

By about 10,000 BC nomadic groups of hunter-gatherers had moved east from the Sahara into the valley of the Nile. At first they probably remained in small groups, moving between campsites depending on the seasons and the annual flooding of the river. They depended on the waters of the Nile and the fertile strips of soil beside the river to provide their food.

Burial and art

The early Egyptians buried their dead directly in the desert sand. The sand's heat dried out the body, helping to prevent decay. Pottery, jewellery, and figurines were sometimes placed around the body. At Hierakonpolis, south of Thebes in Upper Egypt, a large cemetery was built before 3000 BC. It contained a painted tomb which is thought to be the first of its kind in Egypt.

Details from the wall paintings (left) in the tomb at Hierakonpolis. They show large river boats, with many animals and people. These are among the earliest Egyptian tomb paintings ever found.

Farming settlements

By about 5500 BC hunter-gatherer groups started to grow their own crops of wheat and barley. They settled in one place, and before long they were also keeping herds of goats and sheep. These early farmers were able to grow enough to feed themselves and their families, but they were totally dependent on the annual Nile flood to water and fertilize their land.

Villages and crafts

As settlements grew into villages, farmers used the Nile's waters more effectively. They dug canals, which filled when the river flooded and could be blocked off to store the water. As harvests improved, some villagers began to concentrate on other things, such as craftwork. Pottery vessels were fired in simple kilns, and from about 4000 BC they were painted with striking decorations.

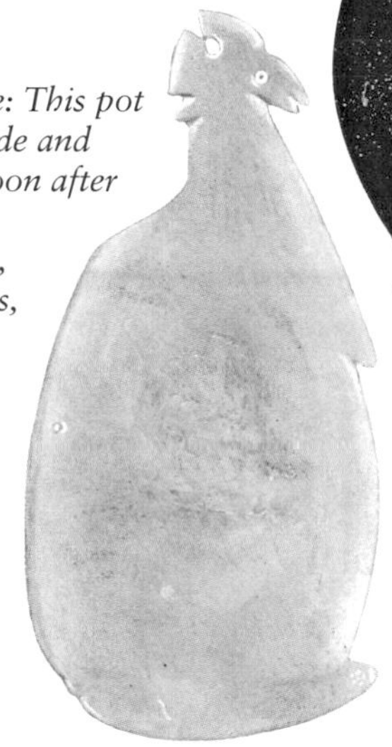

The ancient Egyptians used Nile mud to build shelters and houses. In early times they covered interwoven sticks and reeds with wet mud. For larger structures, they used mud bricks (below). To make these, mud was first mixed with water, then straw and sand were added. The mixture was kneaded together before being squeezed into wooden moulds. The shaped bricks were then turned out and left to dry and harden in the sun.

Above: This pot was made and painted soon after 3500 BC. It shows a boat with oars, cabins, and palm fronds, as well as gazelles, a bird, and a woman.

These animal-shaped stone palettes, with inlaid eyes, were used for grinding cosmetics.

Cosmetics

Both men and women used cosmetics. They ground pigments to make eye-colour, and rubbed ointments and oils into their skin. Cosmetic-grinding palettes and storage containers were made in animal shapes and formed part of people's grave goods.

Right: This ointment container dates from around 4000 BC. Shaped like a hippopotamus, it is made of ivory.

The Nile

The ancient Egyptians called the Nile simply 'the river', and they believed that its floods came from the bottomless water jar of a god called Hapy. The great river meant everything to them. It gave them water and enabled them to produce food, as well as providing a transport route throughout the whole land. They lived on what they called the 'black land', fertile soil produced by the rich, dark silt of the river's floodwaters. Without the Nile, the great Egyptian civilization could never have existed.

Two lands united

The first king to rule both lands of Egypt was Narmer, who reigned from around 3150 BC. He may have been the same king as the legendary Menes, who founded the city of Memphis, which was the new capital of the unified kingdom. On one side of this palette (left), Narmer wears the crown of Upper Egypt as he strikes a prisoner. On the other side, images of lions, a raging bull, and Narmer inspecting his beheaded enemies demonstrate the king's power.

This glazed ceramic fish (right) was used as a flask for perfume.

The calendar

The Egyptians divided the year into three seasons, based on the annual cycle of the Nile. The time of the flood normally lasted from mid-July to mid-November and formed the first season. This was followed by the sowing season, which lasted until mid-March. The last season was harvest time, when the river level was at its lowest.

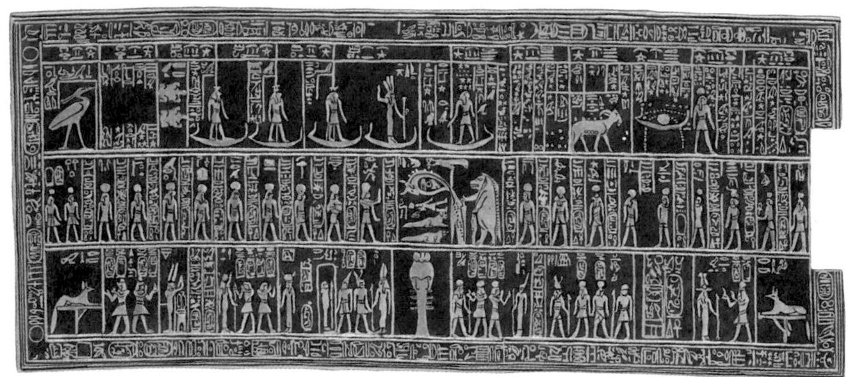

This hieroglyphic calendar (above) shows the seasons in three rows. Each season was divided into four months, based on the moon. A month was made up of three weeks, and each week had 10 days.

Unpredictable waters

The Nile's flood was caused each year by heavy rains in the Ethiopian highlands. These swelled the main branch, called the Blue Nile, which in turn overfilled the main channel flowing towards Memphis and the delta. Dry valleys in the desert (called wadis) also filled after sudden rainfall and flooded surrounding areas. Attempts were made to contain the waters by building dikes and dams, but the forces of nature were too powerful to be controlled.

This dam (above) was built at Helwan, near the east bank opposite Memphis, in 2600 BC. It was made of rubble faced with blocks of stone, and took 10 years to build. Flash floods destroyed part of the dam, however, and it was never finished.

Left: Fishermen used nets, while hunters used spears to catch larger animals such as hippos.

Right: The crocodile-god Sobek wears a distinctive crown. Crocodiles were common along the banks of the Nile in ancient times.

River of life

The Nile was a great source of food, especially fish and water birds, which were caught in nets. Early boats were made from bundles of reeds that grew beside the river. The river's water was used for drinking and washing, and farmers could use only the fertile land beside the river banks for their crops. Houses were also close by, though they were sometimes damaged or washed away when the flood was much higher than usual.

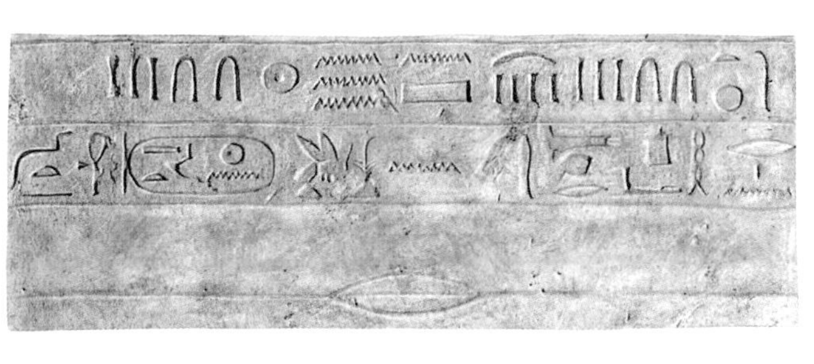

This stela (left) marks the level of the Nile flood in 1831 BC. Farmers were taxed each year according to the level the floodwaters reached and the amount of their farmland that the water covered.

Most ordinary Egyptians lived in villages along the Nile. The river was an important focus of community life – villagers met and chatted as they went about their daily chores along the river banks.

Life in the Old Kingdom

The period of the Old Kingdom began around 2686 BC and lasted for 500 years. The united lands of Egypt came under the rule of four powerful dynasties of kings, who ruled from their capital at Memphis. During this time the country's agriculture and administration flourished, bringing wealth and stability. This encouraged the beginning of great construction projects, including the building of the pyramids. But as always Egypt was totally dependent on the Nile, and towards the end of the period the kingdom weakened when the flood failed for several years.

This statue of King Khafra (reigned 2558–2532 BC) shows him under the protection of the falcon-god Horus. Egyptian people believed that the pharaoh was a living form of the god.

Divine kings

As well as being the human form of Horus, the reigning king was seen as the son of the goddess Hathor. In this statue (right), Hathor stands at the right shoulder of King Menkaure, who reigned from 2532 to 2503 BC. On his left stands another goddess, who represented the 17th province of Upper Egypt. Menkaure was the builder of the third of the famous pyramids at Giza.

The creator-god Ptah (right) was originally a local god of Memphis, where a great temple stood in his honour. Ptah was seen as the patron god of craftworkers.

Memphis

The city of Memphis lay just south of the point where the Nile spread out into the different channels of the delta. This was an ideal location for the capital of the unified kingdom, and the Egyptians called the city the 'balance of the two lands'. The city and its buildings were forced to move over the centuries, as the Nile often changed its course slightly after each annual flood.

This inlaid wooden chest (left) shows the skilled work of craftsmen in the Old Kingdom.

Right: Gilded wooden box full of decorated bracelets. These beautiful items were found in the tomb of Queen Hetepheres I, the wife of Snefru.

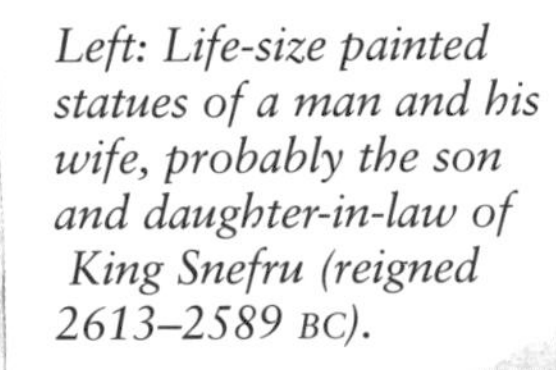

Left: Life-size painted statues of a man and his wife, probably the son and daughter-in-law of King Snefru (reigned 2613–2589 BC).

Officials

The kingdom of Egypt was seen as the personal property of the pharaoh, but many different officials were needed to make it run smoothly and efficiently. The vizier, or chief minister, was the state's highest official. Beneath him were regional governors who ran the provinces, and they were helped by local officials. The officials' most important tasks were raising taxes and finding enough workers to help with major building projects.

Right: Bronze statue of a vizier wearing his official clothing – a long apron kilt with a special strap.

Left: Local officials gave rulings when people broke the law, for example by stealing or not paying their taxes on time. Scribes noted down the judgements. Serious crimes were dealt with at a higher level, by the vizier or ultimately the pharaoh.

Death and the Afterlife

The Egyptians believed firmly in life after death, and they went to great trouble to prepare for this. They preserved bodies of the dead as mummies, so that a person's spirit had a place in which to live on. They believed that, before burial, people were judged by gods, given back their senses in a special ceremony, and then armed with spells for the difficult journey through the underworld. Offerings of food, clothing, and other goods helped the spirits of the dead survive in the afterlife.

An early basket coffin made from bundles of reeds. The body was placed on its side, with legs bent.

Early burial

The first coffins were made from reeds. These were followed by simple wooden boxes, which finally developed some time after 2000 BC into more human-shaped coffins.

These professional mourners were hired to emphasize the grief of a funeral.

Mourning

On its way to burial, a dead body was usually accompanied by two mourning women. Representing the sister goddesses Isis and Nephthys mourning the dead Osiris, the two women stood at the head and feet of the deceased. Other women mourners scattered dust over their heads and beat their breasts in grief, but men rarely showed their sorrow.

This model of servants was put in a tomb to help the dead person in the afterlife.

Tomb offerings

The preserved mummy provided the dead person's spirit with a home in the afterlife. The spirit forms of *ka* and *ba*, which made up the person's 'soul', needed food and drink. The deceased also needed the help of servants, as well as clothing and furniture, in the afterlife.

Below: In the Middle Kingdom period, wooden coffins were often painted with a pair of eyes on the side that faced east. This was to allow the dead person to see the rising sun.

Right: Osiris carries the royal crook and flail. His green skin represents resurrection.

Ruler of the underworld

Osiris, the god of death and resurrection, ruled the underworld. He was present as the dead were being judged. Kings were strongly associated with Osiris after their death, and later so were all dead persons who had passed the judgment of good and evil.

A priest in an Anubis mask holds the mummy, while other priests prepare for the 'opening of the mouth' ceremony.

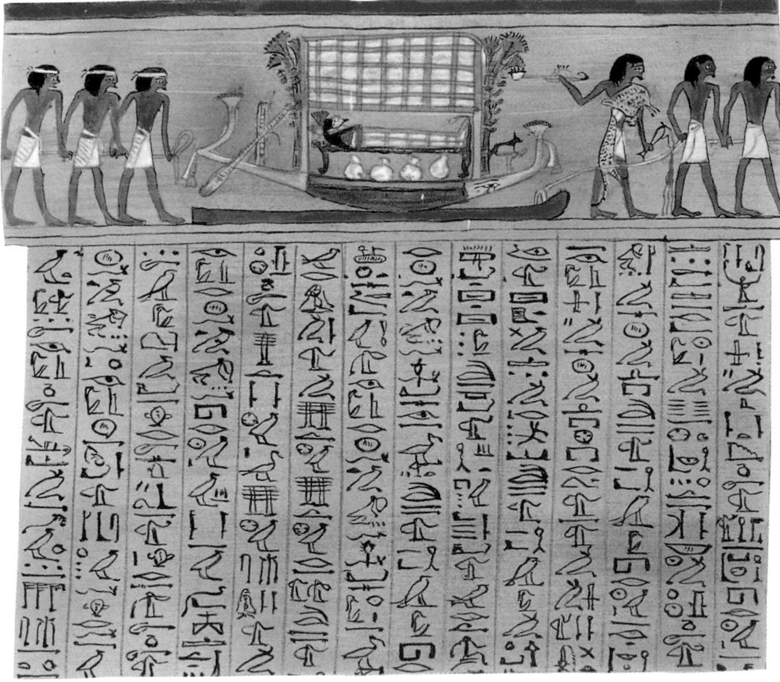

On the way to the afterlife

The Egyptians thought that when they died, their hearts were weighed against the feather of Maat, goddess of truth, in a special ceremony (below). Anubis, the jackal-headed god of thc dead, sometimes tipped the balance in favour of the heart, so that the dead person could pass safely into the afterlife. Before burial, a priest touched the mummy's mouth with a special instrument. This 'opening of the mouth' ceremony was thought to return life to the body, so that the dead person could eat and speak in the afterlife.

Left: A section from the Book of the Dead, found in the tomb of a scribe who died around 1250 BC.

The Book of the Dead

The dead had to travel through the underworld in order to reach the heavenly afterlife. This was a difficult journey, and spells were used to overcome the dangers that would be met on the way. The spells were written on papyrus scrolls that we call the Book of the Dead, and were usually placed in the coffin.

Egyptian Mummies

The ancient Egyptians were experts at mummification – the process of preserving dead bodies and preventing them from decaying. They dried bodies out and wrapped them in linen. The process took time and it was performed as an important, dignified ritual. Mummies were then put inside coffins, and sometimes a stone sarcophagus, before being placed in tombs. In more recent times many mummies were unwrapped to reveal the preserved bodies. Today, archaeologists use special scanners to see inside mummies without unwrapping them and causing damage.

Once the body had been wrapped, a mask was usually placed over the head of the mummy. These masks could be works of art in their own right – often they were stylized faces but sometimes they were more realistic portraits of the deceased. This mummy mask was made early in the 1st century AD, during the Roman period, and it shows the influence of Roman art and fashion. Great care has been taken with the decoration of this mask – it has imitation hair, a glass necklace, and a wreath of delicate blossoms fashioned out of plaster.

Preserving the body

Shortly after death, an embalmer removed the dead person's internal organs, including the brain. The corpse was carefully washed, covered with natural salts, and then left to dry for 40 days. The dried body was packed with linen and aromatic herbs, and coated with oils and resins. Finally, it was wrapped in layers of linen bandages, ready to be put in its coffin. The funeral took place about 70 days after death.

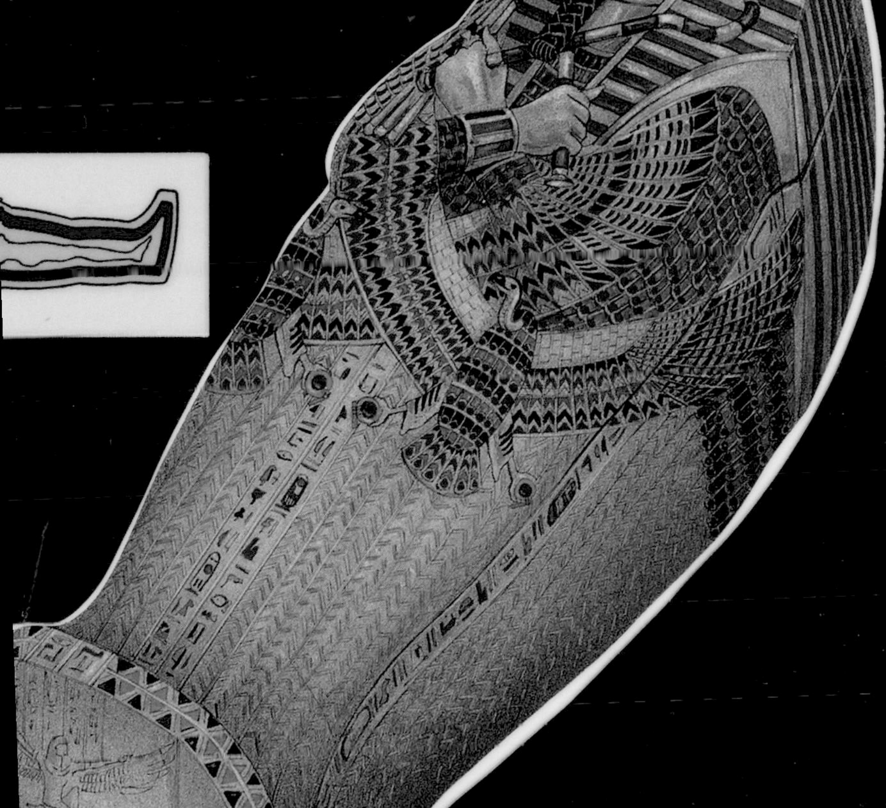

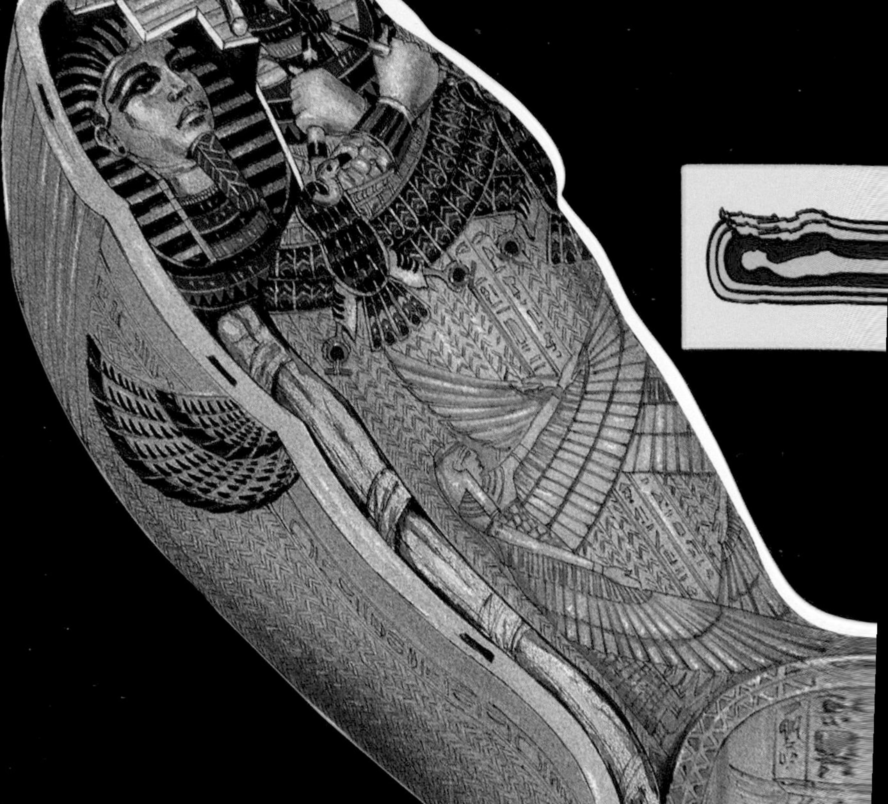

A priest in an Anubis mask holds the mummy, while other priests prepare for the 'opening of the mouth' ceremony.

On the way to the afterlife

The Egyptians thought that when they died, their hearts were weighed against the feather of Maat, goddess of truth, in a special ceremony (below). Anubis, the jackal-headed god of the dead, sometimes tipped the balance in favour of the heart, so that the dead person could pass safely into the afterlife. Before burial, a priest touched the mummy's mouth with a special instrument. This 'opening of the mouth' ceremony was thought to return life to the body, so that the dead person could eat and speak in the afterlife.

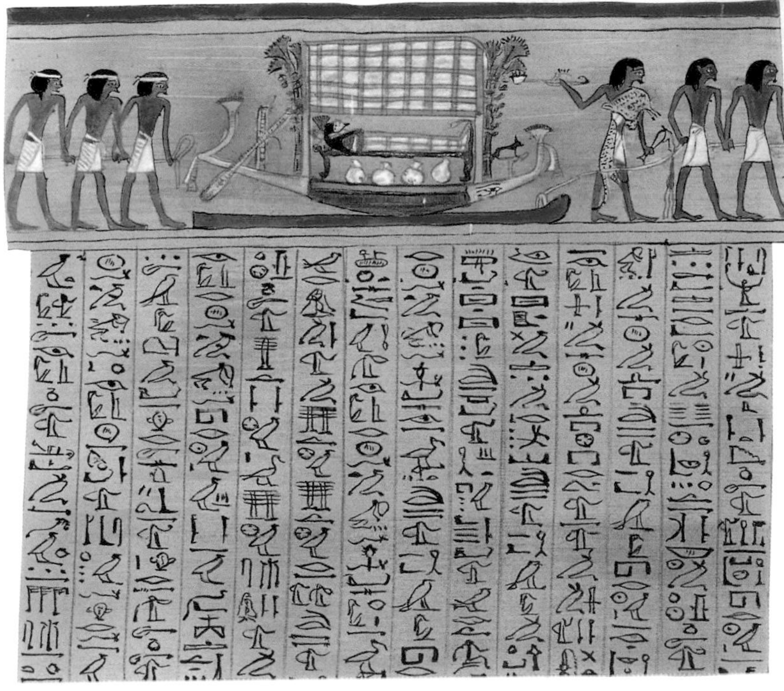

Left: A section from the Book of the Dead, found in the tomb of a scribe who died around 1250 BC.

The Book of the Dead

The dead had to travel through the underworld in order to reach the heavenly afterlife. This was a difficult journey, and spells were used to overcome the dangers that would be met on the way. The spells were written on papyrus scrolls that we call the Book of the Dead, and were usually placed in the coffin.

Egyptian Mummies

The ancient Egyptians were experts at mummification – the process of preserving dead bodies and preventing them from decaying. They dried bodies out and wrapped them in linen. The process took time and it was performed as an important, dignified ritual. Mummies were then put inside coffins, and sometimes a stone sarcophagus, before being placed in tombs. In more recent times many mummies were unwrapped to reveal the preserved bodies. Today, archaeologists use special scanners to see inside mummies without unwrapping them and causing damage.

Once the body had been wrapped, a mask was usually placed over the head of the mummy. These masks could be works of art in their own right – often they were stylized faces but sometimes they were more realistic portraits of the deceased. This mummy mask was made early in the 1st century AD, during the Roman period, and it shows the influence of Roman art and fashion. Great care has been taken with the decoration of this mask – it has imitation hair, a glass necklace, and a wreath of delicate blossoms fashioned out of plaster.

Preserving the body

Shortly after death, an embalmer removed the dead person's internal organs, including the brain. The corpse was carefully washed, covered with natural salts, and then left to dry for 40 days. The dried body was packed with linen and aromatic herbs, and coated with oils and resins. Finally, it was wrapped in layers of linen bandages, ready to be put in its coffin. The funeral took place about 70 days after death.

The dead person's liver, lungs, stomach, and intestines were preserved and stored in containers we call canopic jars (below). Their different lids represented the four sons of the god Horus. The person's heart, which was the symbol of life and seen as the source of human wisdom, was always left in the body.

The sarcophagus

The coffins of pharaohs and important officials were given a further layer of protection. They were placed inside a stone sarcophagus. These rectangular containers were extremely heavy and must have been very difficult to move and place in the tomb. Many were beautifully carved and crafted. Some coffins were put in a rectangular wooden box instead. Tutankhamun's three coffins were inside a stone sarcophagus, which itself was inside four gilded wooden shrines.

This inscribed, mummy-shaped figurine (right) dates from about 1350 BC. Figurines like this, called shabtis, were put in tombs to work for the dead person in the afterlife.

The coffin

A wooden coffin, or mummy case, was used to protect the embalmed body. For added protection, and to show important status, some royal mummies were put inside two or more coffins. The mummy of Tutankhamun, the young pharaoh who ruled from 1336 to 1327 BC, was placed in an inner coffin made of beaten gold. This was put in two further coffins of gilded wood, which fit inside each other like Russian dolls. Valuable objects were placed inside the linen bandages and within the coffin.

Most coffins were highly decorated on the inside as well as outside. They were often covered with images of gods and goddesses, magic symbols, and spells.

The jackal-headed god Anubis was thought to rule over the process of embalming. While a mummy was being prepared, the chief priest wore a mask of Anubis.

Mastabas

Before the age of pyramids, early kings were buried in underground tombs lined with mud bricks and covered with mounds of sand. Later, the tomb was covered by a second mound surrounded by a mud-brick wall, making a structure called a mastaba. These gradually became higher and more elaborate, and further developments resulted in pyramids.

The Giza pyramids

The three main pyramids at Giza, north of the capital at Memphis, were built for King Khufu (1), his son Khafra (2) and his grandson Menkaure (3). Together, their reigns spanned 85 years from 2589 BC. When each king died, his body was brought from Memphis in a funeral boat. The body was mummified in a valley temple beside a canal leading from the Nile. Then it was carried along a causeway to a mortuary temple, before being placed in a sarcophagus within the main pyramid. The king's wives and important officials were buried in smaller pyramids and tombs nearby.

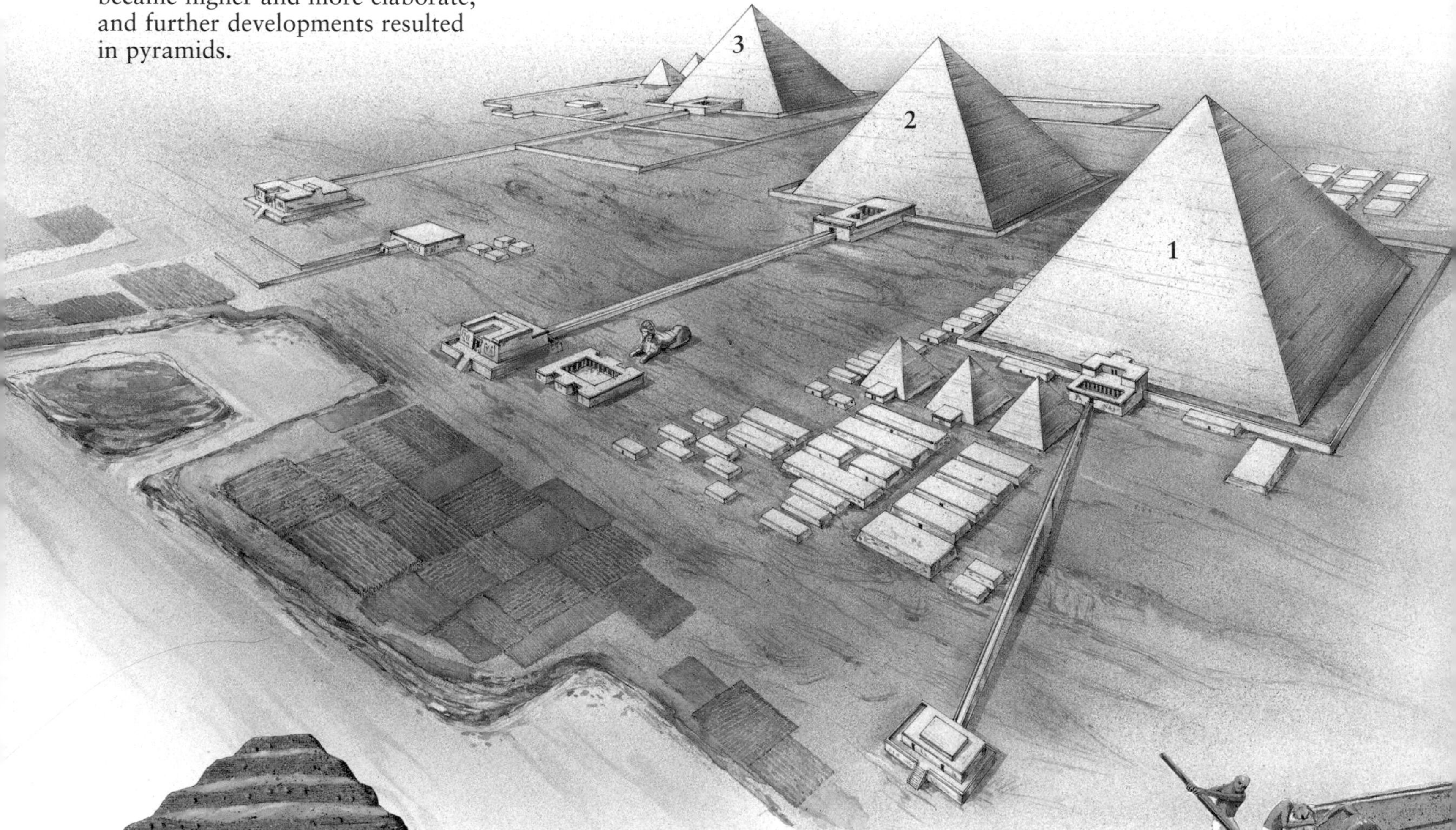

3

2

1

The Pyramids

The great age of pyramid building took place during the Old Kingdom period. It reached its peak with the famous Great Pyramid at Giza, and altogether more than 80 royal pyramids were built in Egypt. These amazing stone structures were built as tombs for pharaohs, serving as sacred places where the dead king's spirit could journey into the sky every day. They were incredible feats of engineering and construction, with huge blocks of stone fitting precisely together. The shape of the pyramids was significant to the Egyptians, as it was a reminder of the original mound of creation and it pointed up towards the sky and the sun.

Early styles

King Djoser's great Step Pyramid (above) was built at Saqqara, near Memphis, around 2660 BC. Inside was a royal burial chamber, with eleven smaller chambers for family members. Other stepped pyramids were built before Snefru built the first two smooth-sided pyramids at Dahshur. One of them is called the 'Bent Pyramid' because its sides become steeper part way up.

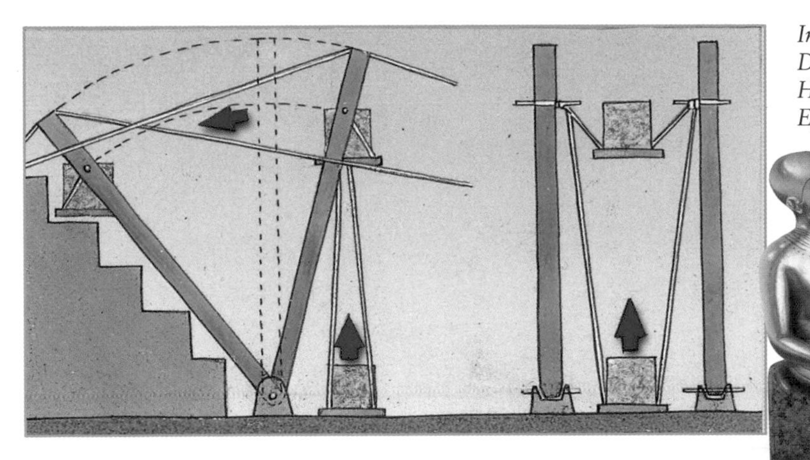

Imhotep was one of King Djoser's most able advisors. He was revered by the ancient Egyptians for thousands of years as an architect, mathematician, astronomer, writer and doctor. He designed and built the first pyramid, the Step Pyramid at Saqqara.

Below: The Great Pyramid of Khufu is 480 feet (147 m) high and measures 750 feet (230 m) along each side of its base. It is the largest pyramid and the oldest of the Seven Wonders of the Ancient World. This illustration shows the interior structure of the pyramid.

Khufu's burial chamber

Entrance

Queen's burial chamber

Secret passage to underground chamber

Building work

It took up to 30,000 men more than 20 years to build the Great Pyramid. They used around 2.3 million limestone blocks, each weighing 2.5 tons or more, and hauled the blocks into place using wooden sledges and rollers. Workers may have built a single supply ramp to one side or narrower ramps winding around the pyramid. Some historians believe they may also have used lifting equipment such as the winch shown above.

Left: King Snefru, the father of Khufu, was the greatest of the royal pyramid builders. He had the first true, smooth-sided pyramid built at Meidum, and followed this with two more at Dahshur. They were built by thousands of workers during the annual floods, when farm work was impossible.

The great sphinx

This massive stone figure has a lion's body with a man's head. Up to 66 feet (20 m) high and 239 feet (73 m) long, the Sphinx stands beside the causeway leading to the pyramid of Khafra. Most historians think it was built during Khafra's reign (2558–2532 BC), and that it shows the king's face. By the time of the New Kingdom, the Egyptians saw the Sphinx as representing the sun-god Horemakhet, or "Horus of the horizon."

The Birth of Writing

Recent discoveries have shown that the Egyptians were using the script that we call hieroglyphs by about 3250 BC, before their lands were even unified. This script used a mixture of word pictures (such as a circle for the sun), sound signs (such as an owl for the letter 'm'), and other symbols. Simpler scripts, called hieratic and Demotic, were also used. They were faster and easier to write. Generally, hieroglyphs were used for sacred inscriptions in tombs and temples, while hieratic (and then, later, Demotic) was used more commonly for everyday purposes.

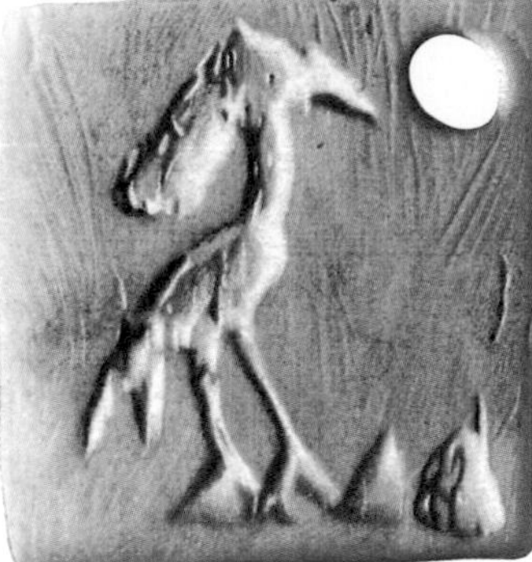

Above: Early hieroglyphs have been found on small ivory and bone labels, such as these. The label with the lightning flash reads 'mountains of darkness', and the one with the ibis 'mountains of light'. They probably refer to the mountains to the west and east of Egypt.

Scribes

Scribes were very important, since fewer than one in every hundred Egyptians could read or write. Many went to work as officials in their local district, while others became architects or clerks to wealthy families. Some scribes worked with the army, organizing supplies and recording daily events. The most important scribes were the scholars and teachers in the temples.

Above: This wooden coffin lid shows columns of beautiful hieroglyphs inlaid with coloured glass.

This scribe (left) is sitting in the traditional cross-legged position. He is holding a papyrus roll with his left hand, and would have had a reed pen in his right. The sculptor has made him look plump, which was regarded as a sign of success in ancient Egypt.

A scribe's wooden palette, with a groove to hold the reed pens.

Tools of the trade

Scribes wrote with reed pens, which they split at the end to make a kind of nib. They mainly used black and red ink, made from soot and ochre, which they kept in limestone palettes. They wrote on papyrus, a material made from the papyrus reed that grew along the banks of the Nile. Our word 'paper' comes from the name of this plant.

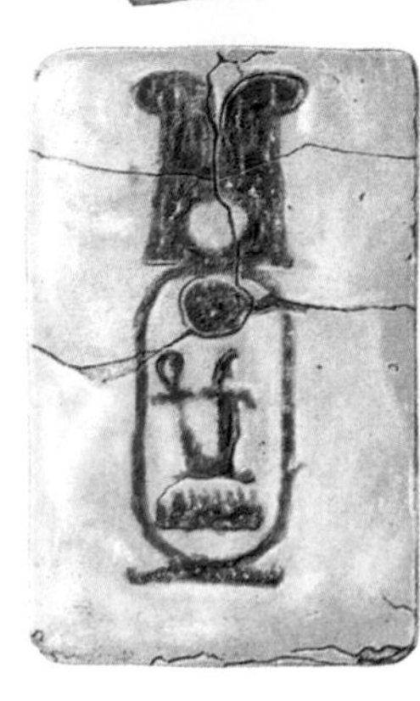

These glazed tiles show the birth and throne names of Seti I, who was pharaoh from 1291 to 1278 BC. The names are placed in oval shapes we now call cartouches.

Learning to write

Only a small number of boys went to school to learn to read and write. They started at the age of five and studied for up to 12 years. They learned hieratic script first, and some then went on to master hieroglyphs. The teacher made them copy words and stories on to pieces of broken pottery or limestone, called ostraca, since papyrus was very expensive.

Making papyrus

The outer part of the papyrus reed was removed (A), and the soft inner pith soaked in water. Then the pith was cut into strips (B). These were laid next to each other, with another set of strips laid at right angles on top (C). The two layers were pounded with a mallet (D), to mash and flatten them together. A weight (E) was put on top while the sheet of papyrus dried out. Individual sheets could be glued together to make a roll.

Left: The Rosetta Stone was inscribed in 196 BC and discovered in the Delta region in 1799. It contains the same text in three different scripts – hieroglyphs, Demotic, and Greek. This allowed the French linguist Jean-François Champollion to decipher the hieroglyphs, which modern historians had not been able to understand before.

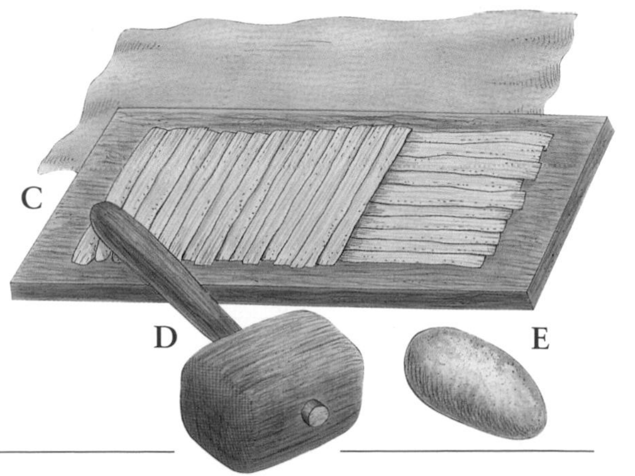

Gods and Goddesses

All areas of Egyptian life were connected in some way to religion – there were gods of the river, of birth and death, of families and learning, and all other aspects of life. The Egyptians believed in many gods and goddesses, and kept small statues of their favourites in their homes. Some were local deities, but others were known and worshipped throughout the land. The gods took many different forms. Most gods were associated with a particular animal, which represented their special qualities such as strength or speed. These gods were often shown with a human body and their sacred animal's head.

In the beginning . . .
According to the most famous Egyptian creation myth, the first god was Amun. He rose up on a mound formed on the waters of chaos, and created a son Shu (god of air) and a daughter Tefnut (goddess of moisture). They in turn gave life to Geb (god of earth) and Nut (goddess of sky). The painting above shows Shu lifting his daughter up to separate the earth from the sky.

Above and right: Thoth in his two forms. As a baboon with the sun's disc and moon's crescent on his head (above), Thoth protects a scribe as he writes. Thoth as an ibis (right) is shown with Maat. Thoth recorded the results when a dead person's heart was weighed against Maat's feather of truth.

Maat: goddess of truth, justice, and the harmony of the world.

Ptah: Creator-god of Memphis, represented as a mummy.

Hathor: Sky-goddess who sometimes took the form of a cow.

Sekhmet: Lioness-goddess whose breath made the hot desert winds.

Khnum: Ram-headed creator-god associated with the Nile flood.

Ra: Hawk-headed sun-god.

Bastet: Cat-goddess who later became associated with the moon.

Sobek: Crocodile-god whose sweat made the Nile.

The household deity Taweret, whose name means 'great goddess', took the form of a pregnant hippopotamus (left). She was thought to protect women during childbirth, and her picture was often carved onto beds and headrests. This statue shows her supporting herself on looped symbols representing the hieroglyph for 'protection'.

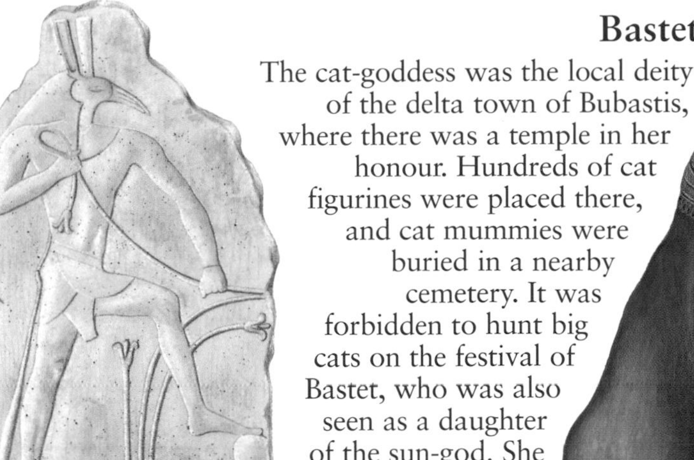

Seth, the god of chaos and confusion, took the form of a mysterious animal with a pointed snout and square-tipped ears (right). The son of the sky-goddess Nut, Seth was supposed to have killed his brother Osiris and then fought his nephew Horus for control of Egypt.

Bastet

The cat-goddess was the local deity of the delta town of Bubastis, where there was a temple in her honour. Hundreds of cat figurines were placed there, and cat mummies were buried in a nearby cemetery. It was forbidden to hunt big cats on the festival of Bastet, who was also seen as a daughter of the sun-god. She is shown in this bronze sculpture (right) wearing the protective eye of Horus on her chest.

Sacred bull

The Apis bull was an individual living animal. It was specially selected according to its markings to be the earthly form of Ptah, the creator-god of Memphis. When each bull died, it was mummified and buried with great ceremony. A new bull was then chosen to represent Ptah.

The dwarf-god Bes (right) was thought to protect family households by scaring off evil spirits. He also kept snakes away from the house.

Local gods

Local gods were worshipped in individual villages, towns, and regions. When a person from a particular god's locality gained power, he often remained loyal to that deity and made him or her powerful too. Important local gods, such as Bastet in Bubastis, had their own temples. Each of Egypt's 42 nomes, or provinces, also had its own regional deity.

Mut: Vulture-goddess seen as divine mother of the reigning king.

Osiris: God of the dead, the underworld, and resurrection.

Nephthys: Sister of Isis who protected the dead.

Thoth: Ibis-headed or baboon god of learning and writing.

Horus: Falcon-headed god represented by the pharaoh

Anubis: Jackal-headed god of the dead and embalming.

Isis: Goddess of motherhood, wife of Osiris, and mother of Horus.

This bronze vessel, called a situla, was used by priests to hold water taken from the temple's sacred lake. The priests sprinkled the holy water during their rituals and at special ceremonies.

Priests

There were several ranks of priests to look after the temple. Many of them never entered the inner sanctuary. Some supervised the temple's workshops, while others oversaw the granaries and slaughterhouses that were needed to provide sacrifices. In order to be clean and pure, priests washed twice during the day and twice at night. They also shaved their heads and bodies.

Priests burned incense and sprinkled holy water to purify the temples and please the gods.

Statue of Anen, the brother of Queen Tiye (c.1410–1340 BC), who was in the rank of priests known as 'second prophet of Amun'. He wears a layered wig, and his priestly outfit includes a panther's skin.

The cult shrine

Each temple contained one or more shrines, or inner sanctuaries, where the golden statues of deities were kept. The shrine was shuttered and secured with a mud seal. The priests would open it carefully each day as they carried offerings of food and drink to the deity. The chief priest removed clothing from the statue of the god and cleaned it, then dressed it again in layers of fresh linen. When he left the shrine, the priest re-sealed the door and swept the floor as he moved away.

Temples and Worship

Egyptian temples were dedicated to one or more gods and goddesses. They were places where priests performed daily sacred rituals for their deities, who were represented by golden statues. The gods were washed, clothed, and fed by the priests in dark, mysterious inner sanctuaries. These were not places where ordinary people came to worship, though people did get the opportunity to see their gods on special festival days.

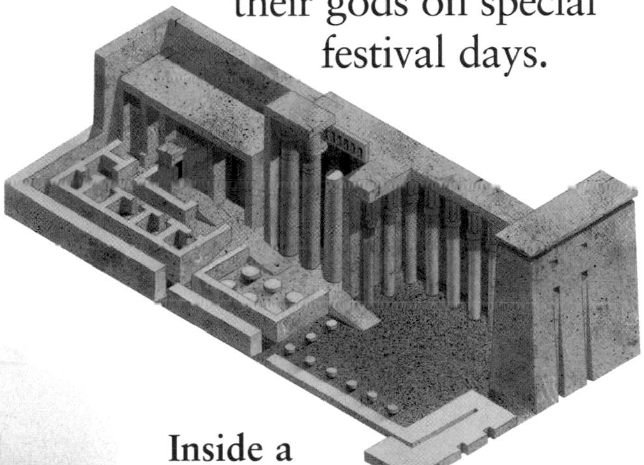

Inside a temple

The main gateway was called a pylon, and it led into an open courtyard. Beyond this was a roofed room with many beautifully carved columns, called a hypostyle hall. As priests walked to the small sanctuary that contained the cult statue of the temple's god, the floor sloped upward and the walls became closer. There was less and less light as priests approached the sanctuary. The temple was a symbol of the universe and its creation.

The temple of the goddess Isis at Philae was built on an island. You can see the two pylons, or monumental gateways, with columns in between them. The last hieroglyphic inscription ever carved in Egypt occurs at Philae.

Festivals

At special times, such as during the annual Festival of Opet and the Festival of the Valley at Thebes, the cult statues of gods were taken out of their sanctuaries. Priests carried them in special wooden shrines, often shaped like boats, to another nearby temple. This gave ordinary people the opportunity to see their gods, and it was a time of great rejoicing.

Agriculture

Most Egyptians worked on the land. They farmed the fertile strips of soil on either side of the Nile, which were regularly flooded. This meant that farmers were very busy for two of the three Egyptian seasons, ploughing, sowing, and then harvesting their crops. Farm work only stopped during the flood season, when the waters spread rich, natural silt across the fields. Farmers worked hard to irrigate their land, making the life-giving floodwaters last as long as possible so their crops would be successful. All this work helped the state of Egypt, since farmers paid taxes according to the success of their harvests.

This statue shows a peasant using a hoe.

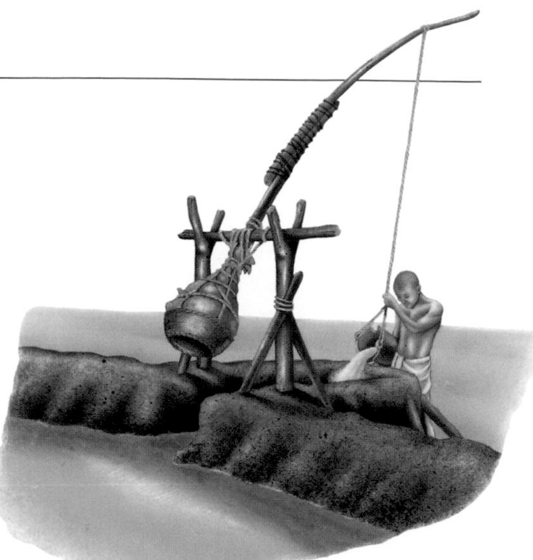

Irrigation

The Egyptians dug ditches and canals off the Nile, so that they could water fields that lay further away from the river. When the floodwaters started to recede, farmers blocked off the canals and stored water for later in the growing season. Workers used a shaduf (above) to move water from the river or from a canal. Shadufs were made from a long wooden pole with a bucket hanging from a rope at one end, and a big weight at the other. The shaduf could swivel around to transfer the water.

Harvest was the busiest time of the year. Wheat and barley were harvested in March or April, and then cattle trampled on the cut stalks to loosen the grain.

This wall painting from about 1280 BC shows an overseer and his wife ploughing and harvesting grain in the 'field of reeds' in the afterlife.

Below: These workers are winnowing – throwing grain in the air and using the wind to separate it from the chaff.

A way of life

Egyptians thought that farming beside the Nile was a good way of life. They respected their life-giving fields, and believed that when they died they would pass through a 'field of reeds'. This field, surrounded by water, was their idea of paradise. They believed that their everyday lives would continue in much the same way during the afterlife.

Important crops

The main cereal crops were barley and emmer wheat. These were used to make bread and beer, the staples of the Egyptian diet. Flax was also grown, and was woven into linen to make clothes. Farmers grew vegetables such as onions, lentils, beans, cabbages, and cucumbers. Fruit grown included grapes, dates, figs, and pomegranates. The fruit and vegetables were usually grown in small, square plots.

Above: Picking grapes in a vineyard. Wine was popular with wealthier people.

Right: This wall painting from around 1400 BC shows harvested grain being measured and recorded. Workers filled jars, which were then emptied into standard-sized sacks to be counted. Scribes recorded the results.

Taxes

Farmers paid taxes according to the amount of crops they produced and the number of animals they owned. In order to calculate this, officials measured fields and counted numbers of cattle, goats, and geese. Scribes noted down how much grain and other food the fields produced. The farmers then had to pay their taxes, often in quantities of grain.

Farm animals

Farmers raised both longhorn and shorthorn cattle for meat, and cows also provided milk. Sheep and goats were reared for their meat, wool, and skin, and were useful for trampling in new seed. Pigs were less common, since they were regarded as animals of Seth, the god of chaos. Geese and ducks were kept for their eggs. Oxen were used for pulling ploughs and threshing grain.

Right: Donkeys carried harvested cereals to the threshing ground and grain to granaries.

Food

Farming, hunting, and fishing meant that food was plentiful in the Nile valley. Generally the diet was based on bread and beer, but there were great differences between the food of the wealthy and the poor. Those who could afford it were able to eat meat, drink wine, and invite their friends to lavish banquets. Ordinary Egyptians were more likely to enjoy a simple meal of fish, along with their bread and beer.

Above: Picking and trampling grapes to make wine. The wine was stored in tall jars, which were often inscribed with the type of wine and the year – just like a modern wine label.

Fishermen would put out their nets in the shallows of the river and then simply haul in their catch. In deeper water, they often spread their nets between two boats.

Fish

There were many kinds of fish in the Nile. Fish was a popular food among ordinary people, and some wealthier Egyptians kept fish in ponds, both to look at and to eat. The pharaoh and priests did not eat fish, however, since it was generally identified with Seth, the god of evil and chaos. Certain kinds of fish were thought of as sacred in some areas and not eaten by anyone.

Baking and brewing

Most women spent a great deal of time at home baking bread and brewing beer. High-ranking wives had servants, but less wealthy women spent much of their day preparing food for their families. Bread was made with flour ground from emmer wheat. Moulds were used to make loaves in various shapes, and bread was eaten with all meals. Beer was made from barley, and later also from wheat. It was a thick brew, but probably not as alcoholic as modern beer. It may often have been flavoured with spices, honey, or dates.

Grinding grain on a stone block, to make flour for bread. Fine stone particles often got into the bread, causing great wear on people's teeth.

Cooking

In order to keep smoke and cooking smells out of the house, food was cooked in clay ovens in the courtyard. Poorer people who lived in a single room cooked over a fire made in a hole in the floor. Food was generally served in pottery dishes, and people ate with their fingers at low tables.

Left: A wooden model showing different kinds of food production. The figures are seen killing a cow, brewing beer, carrying water, grinding grain, and baking bread.

Banquets

Banquets and feasts were often held to celebrate special occasions, like births and marriages. Wealthier Egyptians also entertained friends with food and drink. Cooks prepared a fine meal, which might have included meat, vegetables, and fruit, as well as wine and cakes sweetened with honey. The guests wore their finest clothes, makeup, and jewellery. Some wore pleasantly fragranced incense cones on top of their wigs. They were attended by servants and often entertained by musicians (below).

Meat

Cows, sheep, goats, and ducks were all kept for their meat, and wild animals such as gazelles and hares were hunted for food. Meat was roasted or stewed. Beef was the favourite meat among those who could afford it, but meat was generally expensive and was a special treat for ordinary people.

This wooden model (above) shows a man roasting beef. He is using a fan to boost the fire.

Warfare

The deserts and sea surrounding Egypt provided natural protection against enemies, but the Egyptians were very capable of defending their territory against invasion. They also expanded their empire to the north and the south, believing that the pharaoh had a right to rule all the lands of the world. During the Old and Middle Kingdoms, the Egyptian army was only small. In the New Kingdom, a permanent professional army was created, with charioteers as well as foot soldiers. Military commanders were responsible to their ultimate leader, the pharaoh.

Left: Lion-headed Sekhmet, whose name meant 'the mighty one', was a goddess of war. She was thought to have magical powers and it was believed that she protected the Egyptian king in battle.

This painting shows Ramesses II – who ruled from 1279 to 1213 BC and is known as 'the Great' – fighting the Hittites at the battle of Qadesh in Syria. Ramesses had a large army made up of five divisions of 5,000 men each.

War chariots

Chariots were probably introduced to Egypt from the Middle East soon after 1750 BC. They changed battle methods dramatically. Wooden two-wheeled chariots could each hold two soldiers. A charioteer drove a pair of horses, leaving a trained archer free to fire arrows at the enemy. By the New Kingdom period the king (left, wearing his blue crown) was often shown riding in a war chariot.

Soldiers

The Egyptian army was made up of organized groups of foot soldiers and archers, as well as the later charioteers. There was a northern and a southern corps, and the overall commander was usually a son of the pharaoh. Mercenaries were hired when necessary. The Nubians were excellent archers, and Libyans were often used as infantrymen.

This wooden model of a company of marching foot soldiers dates from around 2000 BC.

This ivory bracer (above) was worn by an archer on his wrist, to protect it from the bowstring when he fired his arrows. The carving shows a pharaoh about to strike an enemy.

Around 1176 BC, the Egyptian warships of Ramesses III defeated the invading navy of the Sea Peoples off the delta coast. This relief commemorates the Egyptian victory.

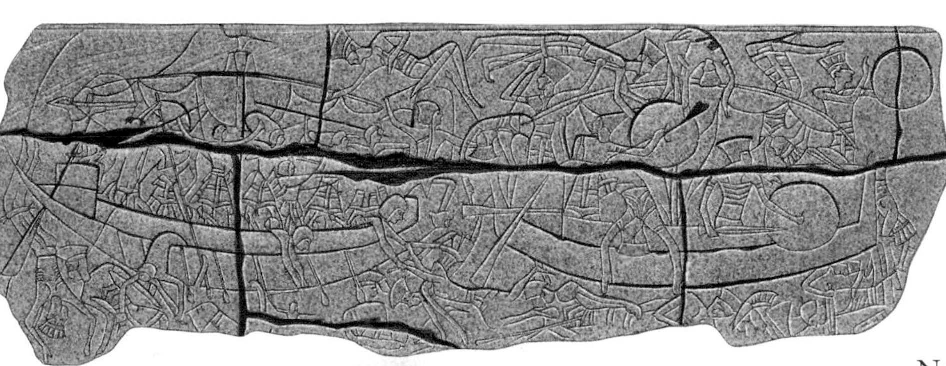

Weapons

Wooden bows and arrows were used by infantry and charioteers. Early arrowheads were made of flint, and these were later replaced by bronze. In close combat, foot soldiers used axes (above) and clubs. By the New Kingdom period swords and daggers were added to the soldiers' weaponry.

Below: This wooden chest was found in the tomb of Tutankhamun. It shows the young king in his war chariot, firing arrows at a group of Nubians.

Egyptian expansion

The Egyptian empire was probably at its largest under the New Kingdom pharaoh Thutmosis I, who ruled from 1524 to 1518 BC. He expanded south into Nubia, which was rich in gold, and gained control of Syria-Palestine as well as much of the Middle East. His grandson, Thutmosis III, continued this work of expanding and protecting the empire through successful military campaigns.

Valley of the Kings

During the New Kingdom period, pharaohs chose to be buried in rock-cut tombs in a deserted valley near the city of Thebes. We call this cemetery the Valley of the Kings, and some queens, nobles, and other family members were buried nearby. The tombs were dug into the hillside, and most are long, steep, and narrow. Despite their cave-like exteriors and small entrances, they were beautifully decorated inside and filled with treasures. Unfortunately, many were discovered by robbers.

This gold necklace was found in the tomb of Psusennes I, who ruled around 1000 BC during the Third Intermediate Period. The tomb is at Tanis, in the Nile delta region.

Tomb robbers

Historians believe that it was because of security problems that the Egyptian pharaohs began to prefer the hidden corridors of rock-cut tombs, instead of the pyramid complexes, for their burials. Entrances were small and probably guarded, while false chambers and concealed steps were designed to lead robbers astray. Nevertheless, most tombs had been looted and emptied of their treasures before 1000 BC.

Left: This painted acacia-wood figure of a vizier comes from an earlier, Middle Kingdom tomb. During that period some important officials were buried in another area of western Thebes, sometimes called the Valley of the Nobles. Their tombs were simpler than those of the later kings, and included a statue of the dead person, sometimes with his wife and relatives.

Tomb treasures

The Egyptians filled their tombs with objects that would be useful in the afterlife. For kings, this included many treasures made of gold and other precious materials. Tutankhamun's small tomb, for example, included three chambers full of treasure, as well as the burial chamber.

Left: This model boat was placed in a tomb to help the deceased on his voyage through the underworld. The model mummy is attended by female mourners.

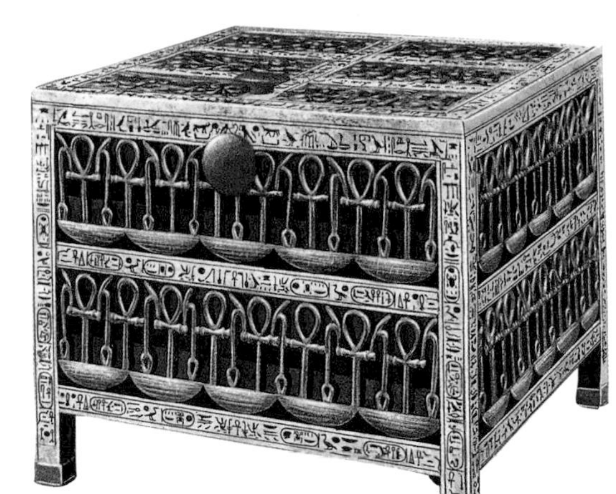

Above: A wood and ivory chest coated with gold and silver, found in a room next to Tutankhamun's burial chamber, which is called the 'Treasury'.

Burial chamber

Steep staircases and long corridors led down to the burial chamber (A), at the end of the tomb. This room contained the mummy of the dead king, in its coffin and sarcophagus, often with many treasures. Along the way to this room there was often a false burial chamber, which was there to try and fool robbers. Behind this was a concealed stairway leading further into the tomb to an antechamber and the real burial chamber.

Tomb decoration

Once a tomb had been cut out of the rock, the wall surfaces were plastered and draughtsmen began designing and drawing images. Masons carved some parts of the designs in relief, before painters filled in the images with their bright colours. Beyond the entrance to the tomb it was totally dark, because it was underground. All the craftsmen had to work by the light of fat or oil lamps.

Above: This painting comes from the tomb of a son of Ramesses III, in the Valley of the Queens. The goddess Isis is leading the prince by the hand.

Women in Ancient Egypt

A woman's main tasks were running the family home and looking after her children. Young women learned to do this from their mothers, and grandmothers often helped their daughters with their families. Many also did hard physical work outside the home. Egyptian women could inherit and own property, and they were allowed to take their husbands to court and divorce them, especially for cruelty. They could not generally hold public office, however, although some did become priestesses. High-ranking women usually had many servants, most of whom were female.

Women from poorer families sometimes took part in farm work, especially if there was a shortage of men to do all the tasks. This woman (above) is scattering seeds on a newly ploughed field.

Queen Hatshepsut (above) ruled Egypt from 1498 to 1483 BC. She had herself crowned 'king' and took the place of her young stepson. Hatshepsut organized major building work, sent trading expeditions, and ordered military campaigns. Some of her monuments show her wearing a royal false beard.

Daily life

Most women's daily lives were spent looking after the home and doing housework. They prepared and cooked food for their families. In wealthier families the mistress of the house had female servants to carry out these tasks (below).

Children

A wife's most important task was raising children. Mothers carried their babies in slings, breast-fed them, and took very good care of them. Girls stayed at home and helped their mothers, learning how to run a household themselves, until they were old enough to marry. Boys spent less time with their mothers, going out into the fields or learning their father's trade from a young age.

Fertility figurines (left) were found in temples, tombs, and houses throughout Egyptian history. Some were offered to the goddess Hathor, the 'lady of the sky' who was thought to be important to the destinies of new-born babies. Others may have represented a woman's wish to be blessed with children.

A woman being helped and protected in childbirth by two representatives of the goddess Hathor.

Marriage

Many girls got married when they were just 12 or 13, and they were usually a few years younger than their husbands. There was no wedding ceremony, but a marriage contract was drawn up. Husband and wife owned all their possessions jointly, but if a man divorced his wife, she kept any valuable items she brought into the marriage.

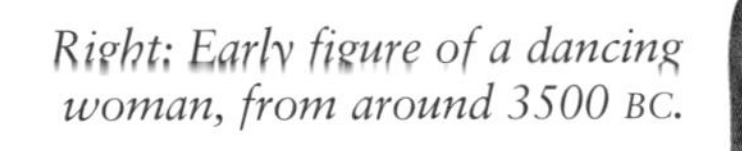

Right: Early figure of a dancing woman, from around 3500 BC.

Occupations

Outside the home, some women worked as bakers or weavers. Others learned to be professional musicians, singers, and dancers, performing at special ceremonies and private banquets. Some women looked after garden plots, growing fruit and vegetables, and sometimes working in the fields. Those from the upper ranks of society sometimes became priestesses and took part in temple rituals.

Above: A priestess wearing the leopard-skin robe of a religious official.

Right: Tutankhamun's wife and queen, Ankhesenamun, anoints her husband with perfume.

Women musicians playing a harp, lute, flute, and lyre.

Queens

Most pharaohs had several wives, but one was always known as the 'great royal wife'. This principal wife was the most important woman in ancient Egypt. Next in importance was the pharaoh's mother, who was held in high respect. Some queens took great interest in the way in which their husbands ran the country.

Clothing and Appearance

The way they looked was very important to the Egyptians. Their clothes were made of linen, which was light, airy, and very suitable for the hot climate. Working men wore simple loincloths or short kilts, while women wore linen dresses. In later times tight-fitting, pleated dresses came into fashion. Both men and women wore wigs, makeup, and jewellery to make themselves look attractive, particularly for special events. As in many other cultures, clothes and general appearance were also a way of showing a person's wealth and social status.

This model shows a servant wearing the typical short kilt.

Fine dresses such as the ones worn by these women (above) were made of the best-quality linen and worn at banquets.

Makeup

Cosmetics were made from various minerals, and both women and men wore makeup. Black eye powder was made from galena, green eye paint came from malachite, red lip paste from iron oxide, and powder to colour the cheeks was made from ochre. Eye makeup may have been useful for protecting the wearer's eyes from bright sunlight. The Egyptians liked to dye their hair with henna, as some people still do today.

This young man (above) is wearing the hairstyle that was most common for boys and girls – the sidelock of youth. Wealthy and important individuals had the sidelock or tress plaited and decorated.

Hairstyles

Egyptian men and women took great trouble over their hair, keeping it clean, neat, and scented. Wealthy households were able to employ hairdressers. Many working men kept their hair short, and there was a great fashion for wigs, which were short for men and longer and more elaborate for women. The Egyptians generally liked to remove hair on other parts of their bodies, both for cleanliness and appearance. They often chose to shave their heads and wear wigs.

This wooden statuette dating from the 19th dynasty (which began around 1300 BC) shows a scribe or dignitary wearing his best clothes, including a long pleated kilt. He is also wearing a layered wig made of small curls.

Left: Wooden boxes such as this were used to store small vases and bottles of makeup and perfume.

Left: These leather sandals were stitched together with papyrus twine.

Linen

Most Egyptian clothes were made of white linen. This came from the flax plants that grew along the banks of the Nile. Men harvested the flax, and then the stems were soaked, to make separating the fibres easier. Women spun and wove the thread into pieces of linen, which were then sewn together to make clothes.

Right: Stems and fibres of the flax plant are shown here in different stages of linen preparation. The fibres were spun on a wooden spindle to make thread.

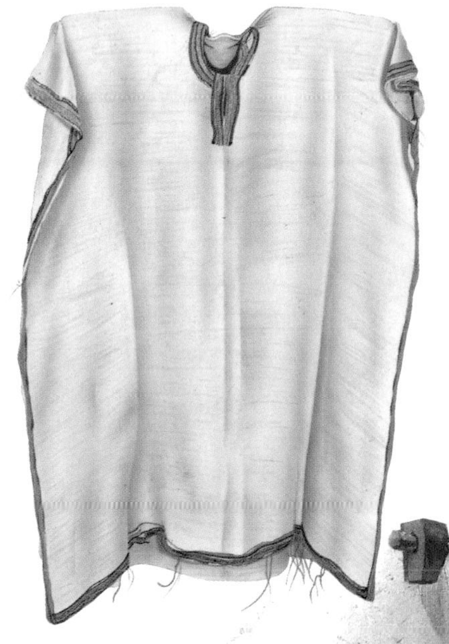

Above: This linen tunic, dating from about 1400 BC, has fine braid trimming.

Weaving flax

Some weaving was done in the home, while larger quantities of linen were produced by a number of women working together to supply big households. From early times they used simple flat looms to weave the flax thread into linen. Later, after about 1400 BC, they used vertical looms, such as the one illustrated below.

By the Middle Kingdom period (beginning around 2040 BC) women were wearing tighter fitting dresses. They also dyed their clothes in coloured patterns, as shown by this offering-bearer.

Fun and Games

Children and adults in Egypt enjoyed many hobbies and activities in their spare time. Men enjoyed hunting and fishing, which were obviously very useful pastimes. Women liked music and dance, and some adopted these as their profession, for entertaining others at banquets and feasts. Adults with enough spare time sometimes sat down to play board games. Children played lots of outdoor games, as well as having toys at home. They also kept household pets.

Above: Queen Nefertari (c.1300-1250 BC) enjoying a board game called senet. Another version of the game (below) has a drawer for keeping the pieces. Players threw sticks or knucklebones to move their pieces up and down the board.

Hunting

Hunting wild animals was a favourite pastime for wealthier Egyptians. The pharaoh himself often liked to hunt big game such as lions (right), and the royal hunt became a symbol of kingship. Hippopotamuses were killed with spears by groups of hunters in the river and nearby marshes (above). Some temple paintings show a hippo being killed by the pharaoh, as a symbol of his power to destroy evil.

Children's games

Egyptian children played some games that are still popular today. Some liked to play soldiers, and some held hands in a spinning dance game. Children played leapfrog and tug-of-war, as well as games of catch with balls made of leather, cloth, or papyrus. These girls (left) are enjoying a game of piggyback.

Toys

Egyptian children played with toys, including dolls and model animals. Some of the doll-like figurines may have been used in adult rituals and as offerings to the gods, as well as in children's games.

These two small figurines (left and right) were carved out of bone.

These two colourful balls were made of leather and filled with seeds to make them rattle.

Below: Wooden toy cat with jaws that were opened and closed by pulling the string.

Pets

Small animals such as cats, dogs, and monkeys were kept as household pets. They were very popular with children. Cats were favourite pets because they killed rats and mice around the home. Some may have been specially trained to help boys and their fathers when they hunted birds.

Left: Figurine of an African monkey.

Music

Some men, but especially women, played a wide range of musical instruments. Instruments appeared very early in ancient Egypt, and some songs have also survived. Music was not written down, but it must have been extremely varied – it was used in religious ceremonies as well as to accompany dancing.

Below: Professional female dancers were very acrobatic. They performed back-bends and hand-stands.

Dance

The Egyptians danced both for fun and as part of ceremonies and rituals. Women often danced at banquets, but no pictures have been found of women and men dancing together.

This woman is playing an early kind of seven-stringed lyre.

Village Homes

Ordinary Egyptian villagers lived with their families in simple mud-brick houses. These were built to stay cool, with small windows, an open-air kitchen, and a roof terrace. There was not much living space and the houses were generally quite bare, with little furniture apart from a few low tables, stools, and beds. In many houses the living room had to serve for eating and sleeping too. Village houses were crowded together, often joining onto each other along narrow streets.

Even large houses presented a blank face to the outside world, with plain plastered walls and small, high windows.

Wealthy homes

Those who could afford it, such as nobles and important officials, had large houses with a central hall, separate bedrooms, and servants' quarters. They had a large courtyard and often a garden, with sycamore figs, date palms, and perhaps even a fish pond.

This model house (left) was placed above a tomb, to receive offerings for the dead. Based on real houses at the time, it has an arched doorway and one small window. A ladder leads up to the flat roof, where Egyptians spent much of their time in the cool of the evening.

Wooden bed-frame, head-rest, and stool, with a blanket and slippers.

Furniture

Ordinary people's houses had little furniture. Low tables and stools were made of wood, and wealthier people had higher chairs with backs. Beds had wooden head-rests instead of pillows, and mattresses were made of rushes. Wooden boxes and chests were used for storage.

Layout

A typical villager's house might have had four rooms, one behind the other. An entrance room from the street led into the living room, which might have had one or two columns to help support the ceiling. Next door was a storeroom, possibly with a cool cellar below. Then there was the kitchen courtyard, with steps leading up to the roof. In these kinds of houses the main room also served as a bedroom, but larger houses had separate sleeping areas. People might also have slept on the roof on hot nights. Most windows were small and high up, to keep rooms as cool as possible.

Baskets, made using coiled palm and papyrus leaves, were very common household items. This basket lid, brush, and low stool (right) were made for use in the home. This particular kind of vase was imported from Mycenae.

Building materials

Villagers' houses were built out of sun-dried mud bricks, and the floors were covered with mud plaster. The walls were coated inside and out with limestone plaster, and some may have been decorated on the inside with paintings. The flat roofs rested on wooden beams. Steps led up to the roofs from the open-air kitchens, where there were usually clay ovens.

A bundle of paintbrushes wrapped in string. At one end, the wood has been beaten so that the fibres act as bristles.

Craftspeople

In Egyptian towns, carpenters and joiners made furniture for the home, as well as wooden models for the tombs of important people. Skilled metalworkers and jewellers used gold and precious gemstones to make items that were beautiful to wear and to look at. The best stonemasons, sculptors, and painters worked for the royal household, decorating the amazing palaces, temples, and tombs that we can still admire today.

Painting

Most painting was done on plastered surfaces. Draughtsmen drew an outline of the picture, which was then coloured in by painters. The draughtsmen then went over the outlines again. Red paint came from a mineral called ochre, blue from copper, and black from soot. White came from lime and was used to lighten other colours.

From very early times jars and other items were made of polished stone at the Upper Egyptian city of Hierakonpolis.

Below: Part of a pectoral made of gold and silver in glass paste.

Jewellery

Egyptian craftsmen and artists made their best jewellery using gold, which was mined in the eastern desert and Nubia. They inlaid it with lapis lazuli, turquoise, amethyst, and other gemstones, to make beautiful necklaces, bracelets, and rings. They also inlaid jewels into wood and glass, and used thin sheets of gold to decorate wooden statues, caskets, and furniture.

Left: Jewellery boxes were put in the tombs of wealthy and important people. This wooden box, inlaid with coloured ivory, contained beautifully crafted pieces of jewellery.

Above: This gold pectoral, or chest ornament, comes from Tutankhamun's tomb. The central scarab beetle, made of a jewel called chalcedony, also forms the body of a falcon. Above it, the eye of Horus wards off evil.

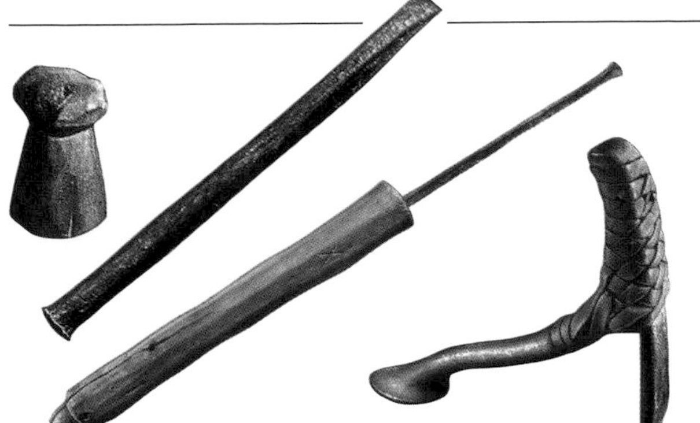

Some woodworking tools: a round burnisher for smoothing pieces down, a bronze chisel, a punch, and an adze with a bronze blade and wooden handle.

Boatbuilders adding wooden planks to a boat.

Woodwork

Carpenters used a range of tools in their workshops. They cut planks of wood by pulling a long saw through the timber, and then shaped the pieces using adzes. Early carpentry tools were made of hardened copper, and later of bronze. As well as making furniture for people's homes, woodworkers carved large statues and made models for tomb offerings.

Metal work

Metals were melted over charcoal furnaces and then poured into moulds. When it had cooled, the metal was hammered into its final shape. From the Middle Kingdom period (2040–1782 BC), tin was added to copper to make bronze. Precious metals such as gold and silver were worked in the same way.

Below: A tomb wall at Saqqara showing scenes from craft workshops. In this scene metalworkers are blowing through pipes to heat metal in a crucible.

The scorpion-goddess Selket (right) was one of four statues that protected the canopic jars in Tutankhamun's tomb. The statue was carved from wood and then covered with gold.

Trade

As their empire grew, the Egyptians began to exchange home-grown grain and papyrus, and homemade linen, for goods they needed from abroad. They bartered for high-quality cedar wood from Lebanon, which they needed to make boats and the best coffins. The African lands of Nubia and Punt provided gold, incense, and other luxuries. Much trade was carried out by boat, but the Egyptians also built forts along desert routes to protect their trading caravans.

These elaborate headdresses were worn by two young Syrian princesses who belonged to the royal harem of Tuthmosis III. The girls were probably given to the pharaoh by a Syrian ruler as part of a peace treaty.

Left: Vase in the form of a Nubian woman.

The Egyptians had been sailing on the Nile since the earliest times, so it was natural for them to use their boats to transport grain, cattle, and other goods. Travel along the Nile, even in boats heavily laden with goods, was made easy by the prevailing winds which blew the boats upstream, and the current, which carried them back down again.

Above: Model of an Egyptian servant carrying the kind of container that was imported from Syria around 1350 BC.

Slaves

Most Egyptian slaves were foreign prisoners of war, and many were owned jointly by communities rather than by individuals. As trade with other lands increased and the Egyptian empire expanded, foreign slaves became more common. They were often forced to work in quarries and mines.

Right: A relief showing men from the land of Punt taking gifts to an Egyptian trading expedition. Punt was on the East African coast, probably present-day Somalia.

Left: The King and Queen of Punt are shown on this relief welcoming the leaders of an Egyptian expedition.

Sea expeditions

The Egyptians went on trade expeditions from the Nile Delta into the Mediterranean Sea. They also carried boats in pieces across the eastern desert to the Red Sea, where they put them together again. They could then sail down the Red Sea to the land of Punt.

Left: A merchant ship under sail.

Right: This alabaster container was used to measure liquids and dates from New Kingdom times (1570–1070 BC). The stone weights were used in the same way as metal weights; lighter ones were made of pottery.

Right: A gilded wooden cubit-rod. The royal cubit was 20.6 inches (52.4 cm) long.

Luxury goods

Gold and amethysts were brought from Nubia, which also acted as a route to the ebony and ivory available in the African interior. Incense, myrrh, and precious oils for use in perfumes and cosmetics came from East Africa and Arabia.

Weighing and measuring

Since coins were not used in Egypt before about 400 BC, metal and stone weights were used to decide the value of things. The basic unit was a copper weight called a deben. Lengths were measured in cubits, which were based on the length of a man's forearm. A cubit was made up of seven palm-widths, each made up of four thumb-widths or digits, making 28 digits to the cubit.

This wall painting from around 1450 BC shows African men carrying live animals and animal skins, as well as ebony, ivory, and ostrich eggs.

Index